THEMATIC UNIT
Colors

Written by Deanna Smith

Teacher Created Materials, Inc.
6421 Industry Way
Westminster, CA 92683
www.teachercreated.com

©2000 Teacher Created Materials, Inc.
Reprinted, 2001
Made in U.S.A.
ISBN-1-57690-616-7

Edited by
Janet A. Hale, M.S. Ed.

Illustrated by
Sue Fullam

Cover Art by
Denise Bauer

Table of Contents

Introduction

Colors has been designed with the early-childhood learner in mind. It is a complete thematic unit for learning color recognition, color as an art element, color for protection, and the basic colors in the rainbow. *Colors* will captivate your children and give them instant success as they explore the colors around them. The core books used for this unit are *Brown Bear, Brown Bear, What Do You See?*; *Mouse Paint*; and *They Thought They Saw Him*. It is filled with a variety of across-the-curriculum activities for the children to enjoy and reproducible pages for the busy teacher.

This thematic unit includes:

❏ literature selections—including summaries of three children's books with related lessons and suggestions for pre-reading, reading, and post-reading activities

❏ writing and language experience ideas—activities geared towards the early childhood learner

❏ poetry—related to the unit topic

❏ planning guides—suggestions for your daily lesson planning

❏ curriculum connections—in language arts, math, social studies, science, art, music, and life skills

❏ bulletin board suggestions—for displaying your children's work

❏ culminating activities—that require the children to synthesize their learning with hands-on experiences and sharing what they have learned with others

❏ a bibliography—suggesting additional literature as well as other helpful resources for materials related to the theme

---

To keep this valuable resource intact so that it can be used year after year, you may wish to punch holes in the pages and store them in a three-ring binder.

Why a Balanced Program?

The strength of a balanced language approach is that it involves children using all modes of communication—reading, writing, listening, illustrating, and doing. Communication skills are interconnected and integrated into lessons that emphasize the whole of language. Implicit in this approach is our knowledge that every whole, including individual words, is composed of parts, and directed study of those parts can help a child to master the whole. Experience and research tell us that regular attention to phonics, other word attack skills, spelling, etc., develops reading mastery, thereby fulfilling the unity of the whole language experience. The child is thus led to read, write, spell, speak, and listen more confidently.

Why Thematic Planning?

One very useful tool for implementing an integrated language program is thematic planning. By choosing a theme with a correlating literature selection for a unit of study, a teacher can plan activities throughout the day that lead to a cohesive, in-depth study of the topic. Children will be practicing and applying their skills in a meaningful context. Consequently, they tend to learn and retain more.

Why Cooperative Learning?

Besides academic skills and content, children need to learn social skills. No longer can this area of development be taken for granted. Children must learn to work cooperatively in small groups in order to function well in modern society. Group activities should be a regular part of school life, and teachers should consciously include social objectives as well as academic objectives in their planning.

Why Big Books?

An excellent cooperative, whole language activity is the production of big books. Groups of children, or the whole class, can apply their language skills, content knowledge, and creativity to produce a big book that becomes a part of the classroom library to be read and reread. These books make excellent culminating projects for sharing beyond the classroom walls with parents, librarians, and other classes.

Why Journals?

Each day your children should have the opportunity to draw, or if appropriate, write in a journal. They may write/draw about a personal experience or answer a general "question of the day" posed by the teacher. The cumulative journal provides an excellent means of documenting children's writing progress.

Brown Bear, Brown Bear, What Do You See?

by Bill Martin, Jr.

Summary

This book has delighted children for years. It is a predictable book that will give children a sense of rhythm and will enable them to read along with you. Eric Carle does the illustrations with his beautifully hand-painted tissue-paper collage.

Below is a suggested plan. Adapt to meet your children's needs.

Sample Plan

Lesson 1

- Use a graphing box to create a bar graph of children's favorite colors (page 6, Enjoying the Book, #3).
- Read *Brown Bear, Brown Bear, What Do You See?*
- Retell the story using story props (page 7, #1).
- Create a child-made book using the brown-bear text patterning (page 6, Enjoying the Book, #2).
- Sing a color song (page 55).
- Make a color treat to eat (pages 57–60).

Lesson 2

- Reread the story while using the story props.
- Complete Who Is Not the Right Color? (page 14).
- Start a "What Do You See?" big book (page 6, Enjoying the book, #3).
- Sing a color song (page 55).
- Make a color treat to eat (pages 57–60).
- Create a Color Sense Poem (page 34).

Lesson 3

- Start the lesson off with an estimation jar experience (page 6, Enjoying the Book, #3).
- Complete My Favorite Colors Booklets (page 7, #2).

- Complete Color Rhymes (page 36).
- Continue your What Do You See? big book.

Lesson 4

- Sing a color song (page 55).
- Complete Color Beginnings (page 35).
- Using a new question, create a graphing box bar graph (page 37).
- Discuss Eric Carle and his tissue-paper illustrations, then make a bear collage (pages 51 and 52).
- Continue your "What Do You See?" big book.
- Sing a color song (page 55).
- Make a color treat to eat (pages 57–60).

Lesson 5

- Reread *Brown Bear, Brown Bear, What Do You See?*
- Conduct a Color Relay (page 56).
- Make Cracker Bears (page 60).
- Finish your What Do You See? big book.
- Discuss how colors are associated with feelings, sayings, and holidays by making Holiday Colors Mini-books (page 7, #5).
- Learn how to say the color names in Spanish or Chinese (page 42).
- Sing a color song (page 55).

Overview of Activities

Setting the Stage

1. To set the mood in your classroom, prepare and display the Great Balls of Color bulletin board (page 69). Reproduce copies of the Messy Day Letter (page 71) to use as needed.

2. Visit the Web Sites (page 77) to learn more about color and to print out available coloring pages for your children to use.

3. Gather books (Bibliography, pages 79 and 80) to place in a viewing area. Be certain to read them first to make certain they are well-suited for your children.

4. Preview videos, software, and music (page 78).

5. Assemble a hands-on graphing box (page 37) to be used for answering daily color questions.

6. Make a set of story props (pages 8–13). After reproducing the props, color, cut out, laminate, and attach them to craft sticks.

7. Prepare an Estimation Jar (page 6, Enjoying the Book, #3).

Enjoying the Book

1. Ask the children to look around the room to see what colors they see. Ask them what colors they see at home. What colors do they see when they play outside? Explain to the children that the story they are going to read is about the colors the different animals see. What is special about the story is that each animal is a different color.

2. Read *Brown Bear, Brown Bear, What Do You See?* Have the children predict what color and animal type each sequential animal will be. After reading the story, provide each child with a copy of page 17. Allow them to fill in the blanks with their favorite portion of the story and then create an illustration.

3. Enjoy one or all of these daily activities:

   - *What Do You See? Big Book*—Write in it daily, using the rhythmic language pattern in the story to eventually create a *Brown Bear, Brown Bear, What Do You See?* children-created version.

   - *Graphing Box*—Use the box (page 37) to ask daily color questions. Here are a few examples:
     - *What is your favorite color?*
     - *What color are your eyes?*
     - *What color is your favorite toy?*

   - *Estimation Jar*—Obtain two large, identical glass jars. Place them both in view of the children. In one jar, place 10 edible items. Place the same items in the second jar, until the jar is completely full. Have the children first look at the 10-item jar to help them make an estimation of the amount in the identical second jar. Allow them to share their estimations. Record their answers on chart paper. Now count the items in the second jar. Draw some conclusions, then enjoy eating the counted items as a snack.

     Some colorful examples for the estimation jar:

     - Red—red jellybeans
     - Brown—chocolate kisses
     - Yellow—lemon drops
     - White—mini-marshmallows
     - Orange—fish-shaped crackers
     - Black—cut-up black licorice
     - Green—grapes
     - Blue—blueberries
     - Purple—grapes

   - *Color Order*—Line up the children in a "human bar graph" that represents the dominant color of clothing being worn. Discuss the results in mathematical terms. If time allows, line them up based on their clothing from the lightest to darkest color and/or the darkest to lightest color.

Overview of Activities *(cont.)*

Extending the Book

1. If you have not pre-made the story props, have the children color and cut out their own story prop sets (pages 8–13). When they are finished cutting them out, have them attach the props to craft sticks with tape or glue. Then have them retell the story to a friend.

2. Ask the children to name some of their favorite color items. Have them draw these items in reproduced and assembled My Favorite Colors Booklets (pages 15 and 16). To assemble, cut out and fold on lines; crease lines well. Place page 16 inside of page 15; staple together on the left side edge. Then, using color-coated chocolate candies, provide a random handful to each child and allow your children to graph their candies using reproduced copies of page 39.

3. Allow the children time to practice spelling their names using colored construction paper. Write each child's name on a strip of construction paper. Cut apart each name letter-by-letter and place in an envelope. Let the children take turns spelling their names, as well as their friends' names.

4. Colors are associated with different meanings, sayings, sports teams, school colors, and holidays. Have the children draw and/or write about one or all of these color associations.

   Some color meanings are:

   - *Red means anger, embarrassment, or danger.*
   - *Orange means bravery or sunshine.*
   - *Yellow means fear, caution, or happiness.*
   - *Green means envy or illness.*
   - *Blue means icy and cold or sad and lonely.*
   - *Purple means royalty or hurt feelings.*
   - *Pink means good health.*

   Some color sayings are:

   - *Once in a blue moon.*
   - *Red as a rose.*
   - *White as snow.*
   - *Feeling blue.*
   - *You have a green thumb.*

5. Ask the children to think of a holiday they enjoy and to think about what colors they associate with that holiday. Discuss how we associate colors with certain holidays. Reproduce the Holiday Colors Mini-book (pages 44–49), one per child. After reading the book with the children, allow them to color it and take it home to share with their families.

6. Have the children dictate how they would cook their favorite "colored" food. Record their responses exactly as they tell you. Write out their recipes and have them illustrate their favorite foods. Reproduce, collate, and send the recipes home as special gifts.

7. Explain to your children Eric Carle's collage technique (page 52) or watch his video (page 78), especially where he shows you how he created the illustrations for *The Very Hungry Caterpillar.*

Brown Bear Story Props

8

Brown Bear Story Props *(cont.)*

Brown Bear Story Props *(cont.)*

10

Brown Bear Story Props *(cont.)*

Brown Bear Story Props *(cont.)*

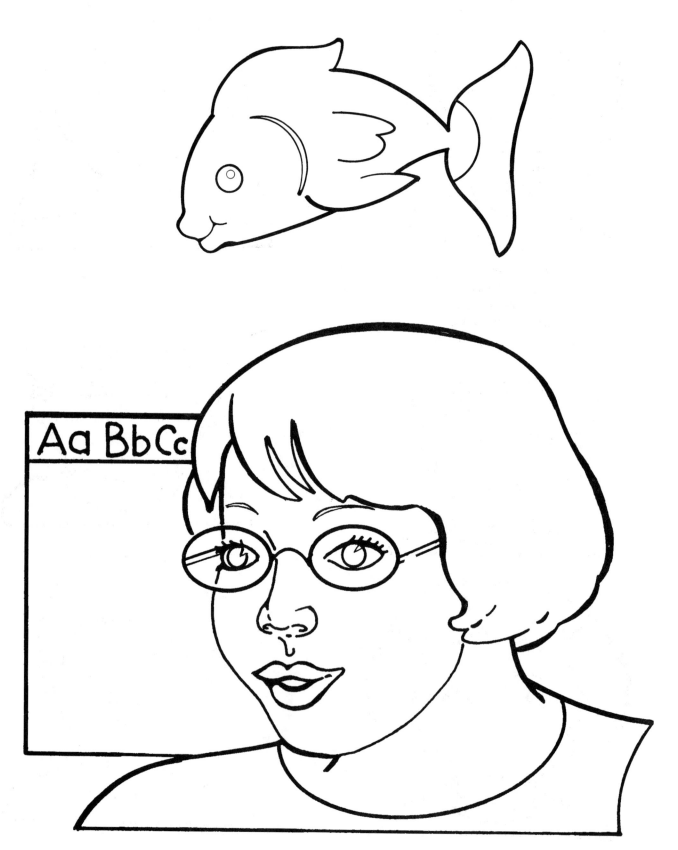

12

Brown Bear Story Props *(cont.)*

Who Is Not the Right Color?

Color the animals. Circle the animals that are not really that color.

Brown	**Red**	**Yellow**
Blue	**Green**	**Purple**
White	**Black**	**Orange**

My Favorite Colors Booklet

Black

Red

Purple

My
Favorite Colors
Book

by
_____

My Favorite Colors Booklet *(cont.)*

Orange

Blue

Yellow

Green

What Do You See?

_____, _____,

What do you see?

I see a _____ looking at me.

Brown Bear

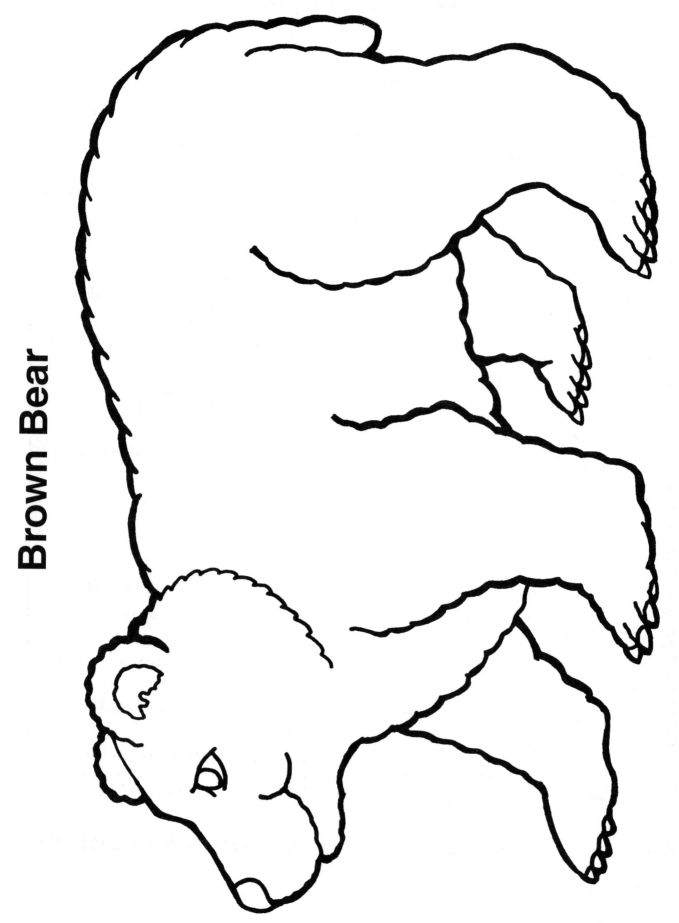

Mouse Paint

by Ellen Stoll Walsh

Summary

Three white mice hiding from a cat find three jars of paint. They get into one of each of the jars of paint (red, yellow, and blue) and discover they can have fun in the puddles left behind.

Below is a suggested plan. Adapt to meet your children's needs.

Sample Plan

Lesson 1

- Have your children decorate created art portfolios (page 74).

- Read *Mouse Paint*.

- Use color paddles (page 20, Setting the Stage, #3) to discuss the basic color wheel concepts (page 20, #4).

- Make color-wheel paper chains (page 21, Enjoying the Book, #5).

- Create Primary Mice Patterns (page 22).

- Read a color poem (page 32).

- Sing a color song (page 55).

Lesson 2

- Reread *Mouse Paint*.

- Enjoy painting by numbers (page 21, Enjoying the Book, #6).

- Create a Color Splash (page 41).

- Play with some Colorful Water (page 41).

- Play the Color Wheel game (page 56).

- Eat a colorful treat (pages 57–60).

- Read a color poem (page 32).

- Complete the Rainbow Match (page 38).

- Sing a color song (page 55).

Lesson 3

- Discuss the concept of the color wheel (page 76). Make Secondary Hand Prints (page 53).

- Make Complementary Paper Weaving mats (page 54).

- Complete the Lightest to Darkest and Mixing Tints and Shades activities (page 50).

- Make monoprints (page 21, Extending the Book, #5).

- Sing a color song (page 55).

Lesson 4

- Discuss natural color dyes and dye small pieces of yarn or cloth (page 21, #7).

- Discuss the last page of the book (page 21, #8).

- Enjoy one more poem, song, and tasty treat (pages 32, 55, and 57–60).

- Enjoy rainbow colors, indoors and out (page 40).

- Have children share their art portfolios (finished art work) and award them all with ribbons and bookmarks (page 72).

Overview of Activities

Setting the Stage

1. Familiarize yourself with a variety of color concepts by reading Color Basics (page 74), Color and the Wheel (page 76), visiting the Sanford Web site (Web sites, page 77), and *A Color Sampler* (Bibliography, page 80).

2. Reproduce, cut out, and assemble the portfolios (page 74), one portfolio per child. Have the children decorate their portfolios which will be used to hold their artwork.

3. Make color paddles. Homemade color paddles are made using colored cellophane and tagboard. Reproduce three copies of the paddle (right) onto tagboard. Cut out the paddles, as well as the paddles' centers. Cut out a blue, red, and yellow piece of cellophane, just slightly larger than the paddle's cut out center. Attach each cellophane piece to a paddle using transparent tape, taping the cellophane to each paddle's frame.

Enjoying the Book

1. Read *Mouse Paint*. Have the children predict what colors will be made when the mice play with the paint.

2. Discuss how the artist used cut paper collages to make the illustrations. Have your children try to make a mouse using the same technique.

3. Read *The Art Box* (Bibliography, page 79) and talk about an artist's tools: portfolios, palettes, paint brushes, and art boxes.

4. Discuss the concept of a color wheel (page 76). Complete page 23 as a class.

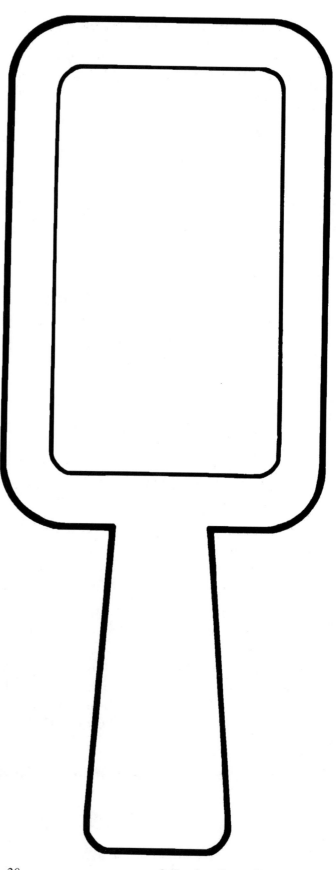

Overview of Activities *(cont.)*

Enjoying the Book *(cont.)*

5. Make a color wheel paper-chain. Cut thin (1" x 8"/2.54 cm x 20 cm) red, orange, yellow, green, blue, and purple construction-paper strips. Staple the red strip ends together. Add the orange strip by placing it through the center of the red strip. Staple the orange strip to start the chain. Continue using the colors in this order: yellow, green, blue, and purple. Lastly, connect the purple to the beginning red strip.

6. Use purchased watercolors to mix the primary colors and paint reproduced copies of page 24. (Note: For very young children, use crayons instead.)

Extending the Book

1. Reread *Mouse Paint*. Have your children role-play the mouse characters.

2. Have your children color the mice on reproduced copies of page 22 and create pattern sequences by gluing their colored mice to sentence strips.

3. Create paper weavings using complementary colors (page 54). Let the children choose which colors they would like to use for the paper weaving. Their choices need to be red/green, blue/orange, or yellow/purple.

4. Enjoy the art activity Lightest to Darkest (page 50).

5. Make shades and tints with your children using a medium known as monoprints. You will need laminated pieces of 9" x 12" (23 cm x 30 cm) construction paper, tempera paint, paintbrushes, toothpicks, 9" x 12" (23 cm x 30 cm) white construction paper, and rolling pins. The children begin by first applying small amounts of paint to the laminated paper using the paintbrushes. With toothpicks, they now draw their illustrations in the applied paint. Place a piece of white construction paper over each child's illustration; roll over it with the rolling pin. Remove the white paper and the printed design will appear!

6. Explain the concept of color tones (page 76). Make gray paint by mixing black and white tempera paint. Discuss the results. Have the children add a dab of the blended gray paint to their favorite tempera paint color to create a toned color.

7. Read *Charlie Needs a Cloak* (Bibliography, page 79). Discuss how dyes can be made chemically or by using nature's fruits or vegetables. Gather some fruits (blueberries, blackberries, prickly pear fruit, etc.) or vegetables (beets, spinach leaves, onion skins, etc.) from your local market or an open field. Fill a medium-sized pot with your chosen food item; just cover the food with water and simmer for about two hours. Drain the liquid into a bowl, straining out any remaining fruit or vegetables. Dye small strands of cotton yarn or cloth in the natural dye solution by soaking overnight. Use the dyed pieces for a display or an art project.

8. Discuss the last page *Mouse Paint* with your children. Ask them, "Why did the mice leave a part of the wall white?" This will bring up the idea of camouflage. Camouflage is discussed during the reading of *They Thought They Saw Him* (page 25).

9. Host an art show displaying your children's art made during this unit. Hand out My Personal Best! ribbons and reading bookmarks (page 72).

Primary Mice Patterns

Color three mice red, three mice yellow, and three mice blue. Cut out the mice. Make a mice pattern.

Mouse Color Wheel

Color the mice.

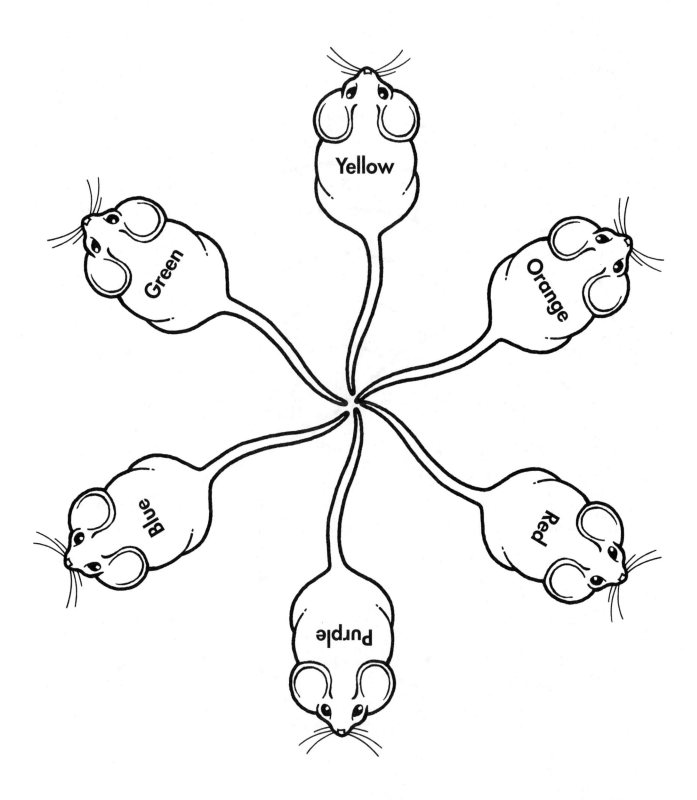

Paint by Number

1–Red   2–Orange   3–Yellow   4–Green   5–Blue   6–Purple   7–Brown   8–Gray

They Thought They Saw Him

by Craig Kee Strete

Summary

A little American chameleon (anole) takes his first walk after a long winter's rest. As he walks, he looks for bugs to eat. His colors change to help him avoid being eaten.

The outline below is a suggested plan for using the activities presented in this unit.

Sample Plan

Lesson 1

- Familiarize your children with the concept of camouflage (page 26, Setting the Stage, #2).
- Read *They Thought They Saw Him.*
- Create camouflage colors (pages 26, Enjoying the Book, #1).
- Complete I Like Colors! (page 33) by having the children (one sheet per child) fill in the blanks.
- Learn colors in American Sign Language (page 43).
- Eat a colorful treat (pages 57-60).
- Sing a color song (page 55).

Lesson 2

- Re-read or re-visit the illustrations in *They Thought They Saw Him.*
- Discuss what a reptile is (page 26, Enjoying the Book, #2).
- Complete the Lizard Match (page 30).
- Discuss how animals use camouflage for protection and to capture prey (page 26, Extending the Book, #1).

- Play a predator and prey game (page 27,#4).
- Sing a color song (page 55) or recite a color poem (page 32).

Lesson 3

- Re-look at the anole in the story's illustrations. Discuss the difference between a chameleon and an American chameleon (page 26, Extending the Book, #3).
- Discuss how people use colors for protection (page 27, #5).
- Create a big book "Special Colors," which contains child-illustrated pages showing protection-colored items (e.g. yellow school bus, red and white stop or yield sign, etc.).
- Eat a colorful treat (pages 57-60).
- Sing a color song (page 55).

Lesson 4

- Conduct the Color Day Celebration (pages 61-67).
- Pass out color certificates (page 71).

Overview of Activities

Setting the Stage

1. Learn about camouflage by reading the nonfiction books, page 80, and by viewing the videotapes *Animal Colors* and *Reptiles and Insects* (view the reptiles portion only), page 78. (Note: Discuss with the children that many people think that chameleons change their colors to match their surroundings. This is not true. Chameleons change their colors as a reaction to their emotions, such as scared or surprised, and temperature variations.)

2. Ask your children if they have ever been told not to wear certain colors at night? Why might that be? Discuss the concept of camouflage. Discuss the ways that animals use color to protect themselves.

3. Read *They Thought They Saw Him*. Allow the children to predict what color the chameleon will turn as the story unfolds.

Enjoying the Book

1. Re-visit the story, focusing on the illustrations and how the chameleon hid itself. Have the children paint using camouflage colors (pages 28 and 29). The children will use small scrap sponge pieces and green tempera paint to sponge-paint the chameleon and the leaves. Cut out the painted chameleon and glue it on top of the painted leaves.

2. Explain what a reptile is. Their main characteristics include: they are cold-blooded; they have rough, dry skin; most lay eggs; and they have a backbone. Explain to the children that there are many kinds of lizards. Have the children complete the Lizard Match (page 30).

Extending the Book

1. Discuss how animals use their colors to hide from their enemies and to capture their prey. The chameleon, for example, has a swaying motion to its walk. This movement causes animals to think it is a leaf and helps it avoid being eaten by predators. The zebra uses its stripes to confuse predators, while other animals use their own special markings to confuse predators. Some animals use their colors to blend into their surrounding so that they can catch their dinner without being seen. Complete Animal Colors (page 31).

2. Make a copy of the chameleon (page 28) using the same color of construction paper as you did for one of the bulletin-board gumballs (page 69); cut out. Attach the chameleon to a pointer stick. Show the children how it can use its color to blend in with its surroundings as you place it against the various colors of gumballs on the bulletin-board display.

3. Make a Venn Diagram to discuss the differences between an American chameleon and a chameleon. The chameleon in *They Thought They Saw Him* is an anole, also known as an American chameleon. Chameleons are most commonly from the forest regions of Africa and the island of Madagascar. Anoles live in the Southeast states of the United States, Central America, and South America. The chameleon has special features that the anole does not have. Chameleons have prehensile tails, which means they use their tails to grasp limbs to hold themselves in place. Anoles can do something chameleons cannot—grow back their tails if lost. Chamelon's eyes move independent of one another so that they can look in front and in

Overview of Activities *(cont.)*

Extending the Book *(cont.)*
---

back simultaneously. The chameleon body is flat on the sides with a large head. The anole has a slender body and a long tail. Both lizards are mostly diurnal, which means they are active during the day and sleep at night. Both are carnivores, with their main staple being insects.

4. Play a predator and prey game. Divide your children into two equal groups. One group will be the predators and the other the prey. Determine an area wherein the children can hide plastic lizards. (The children who are the predators close their eyes while the prey hide the lizards.) After the children hide the lizards, the predators search for their "food."

5. Emergency vehicles use colors to help protect themselves and others. Brainstorm ways people use colors for protection. For example, fire trucks are a bright red color to warn others. Safety signs are different colors—red stop signs, red and white yield signs, tri-colored traffic lights, and yellow school signs. People wear special clothing to blend in with their surroundings in the armed services. Some children and school staff wear school colors one day a week to show school spirit and pride. Explain that sometimes wearing certain colors is a way that people show their support for their favorite sports team. Ask the children to think of their favorite sport. Ask them what colors their favorite teams wear. For the next week, ask the children to wear a specific color, or combination of two colors per school day. Close this discussion by reciting the poem "I Wore the Colors of the Rainbow" (page 32).

6. Conduct the Color Day Celebration (pages 61-67).

Camouflage Colors

Camouflage Colors *(cont.)*

Lizard Match

Match the lizards to the number.

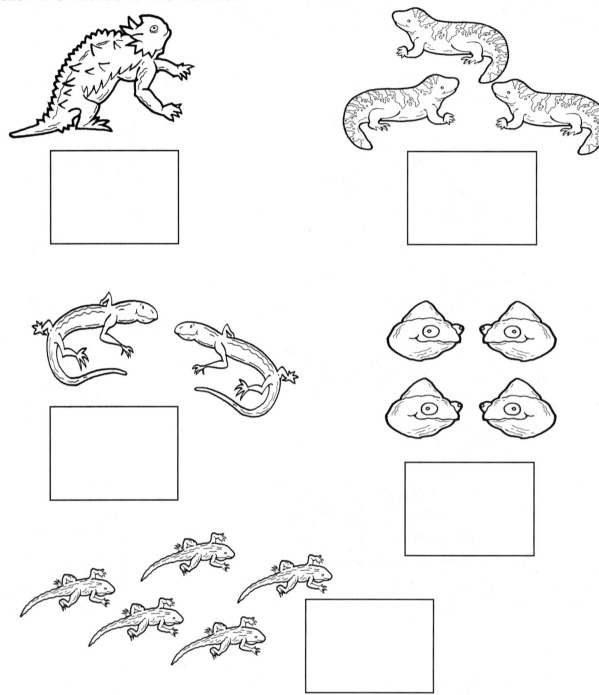

Cut and paste.

| 1 | 2 | 3 | 4 | 5 |

30

Animal Colors

Animals use their colors and special markings to hide from their enemies or to catch their prey. Match the animal to its habitat.

Color Poems

I See Colors All Around Me

These are colors I can see,
They are all around me.
White fluffy rabbits, gentle black bats,
Glowing orange pumpkins, furry brown cats.
Nice green grass, big yellow sun,
Bright blue sky—it's so much fun!

I Am An Artist

I paint things that I can see,
Like red in a sunset sky and oranges in a tree.
Yellow bananas way up high,
Green frogs and a wonderful blue butterfly.
Purple grapes and a ripe red apple.
With my paintbrush I can dapple,
A little paint here, a little paint there.
Colors, colors, they're everywhere!

I Wore the Colors of the Rainbow

On Monday, I wore a red sweater that came up to my chin.
On Tuesday, I wore a pair of orange socks that made me grin.
On Wednesday, I wore a yellow shirt that looked like the sun.
On Thursday, I wore green pants. That was fun!
On Friday, I wore a blue scarf—the color was just right.
On Saturday, I wore a purple cap and my friends said, "You are out of sight!"
On Sunday...I wore all the colors of the rainbow.

They Are Out There Hiding

If you look hard you can see,
Animals hiding from you and me.
They hide on land and in the deep blue sea,
Some look like brown twigs high up in a tree.
If you do see them, please remember this rule,
Do not touch, they need to go to school!

I Like Colors!

I Like _____

by _____

_____ is a color that like.

I wear _____ when I hike or bike.

I look for _____ things all around.

Here are some _____ things I have found:

_____ is my favorite _____ toy.

When I play with it, it brings me joy!

Color Sense Poem

_____

(color)

_____

By

_____ looks like _____.

_____ sounds like _____.

_____ feels like _____.

_____ tastes like _____.

_____ smells like _____.

Can you sense my color?

Draw something using your color.

Color Beginnings

Use the letters to make color words. Match the color to the correct picture by drawing a line.

bl		o		r		p		y
	gr		br		wh		bl	

__own   bat

__ed   snowflake

__ellow   cherries

__ue   bear

__een   pumpkin

__urple   bluebird

__ite   banana

__ack   leaf

__range   grapes

Color Rhymes

Color the circles. Draw a line to match the color word and its rhyme. Now color the matching pictures.

Brown	◯		glue
Red	◯		hay
Yellow	◯		kite
Green	◯		bed
Blue	◯		queen
Black	◯		fellow
White	◯		clown
Gray	◯		backpack

Graphing Box

Set aside a time during each day of this unit to graph important information from your children's lives. Use the graphing box (materials and directions below) to graph the desired information. Graph "real-life" information such as favorite colors and colored items such as toys, foods, fruits, vegetables, crayons, shoes, etc. Help the children to mathematically interpret the bar graphs.

Materials

- empty and washed out one pint (600 mL) milk cartons (one per child)
- white butcher paper
- scissors
- rubber cement
- crayons
- cardboard box, approximately 3' x 2' x 6" (91 cm x 61 cm x 15 cm)
- permanent marker
- tape
- self-sticking notes
- 11" x 11" (28 cm x 28 cm) tagboard
- dry-erase marker

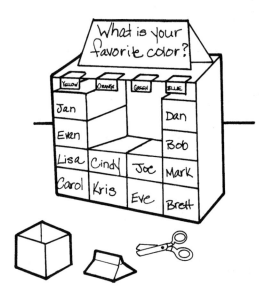

Directions

1. Cut the milk carton spout off to create a rectangular box.

2. Cover the outside of the box with white butcher paper (use the rubber cement to attach the paper to the box). Allow the children to decorate their boxes with the crayons.

3. Use the permanent marker to label the bottom of the milk carton with each child's name.

4. Cover the large cardboard box, inside and out, with white butcher paper; glue into place.

5. Turn the box on its side. Use the sticky notes to create column headers by sticking them to the top of the box to form columns. (You will be changing the column headings daily.)

6. Fold the tagboard in half to make a tent. Unfold and laminate; re-fold. Write your desired "color question of the day" on the tent with the dry-erase marker.

7. To use, have the children place their decorated milk cartons under the answer column of their choice.

Rainbow Match

Match the number clouds to the correct raindrops.

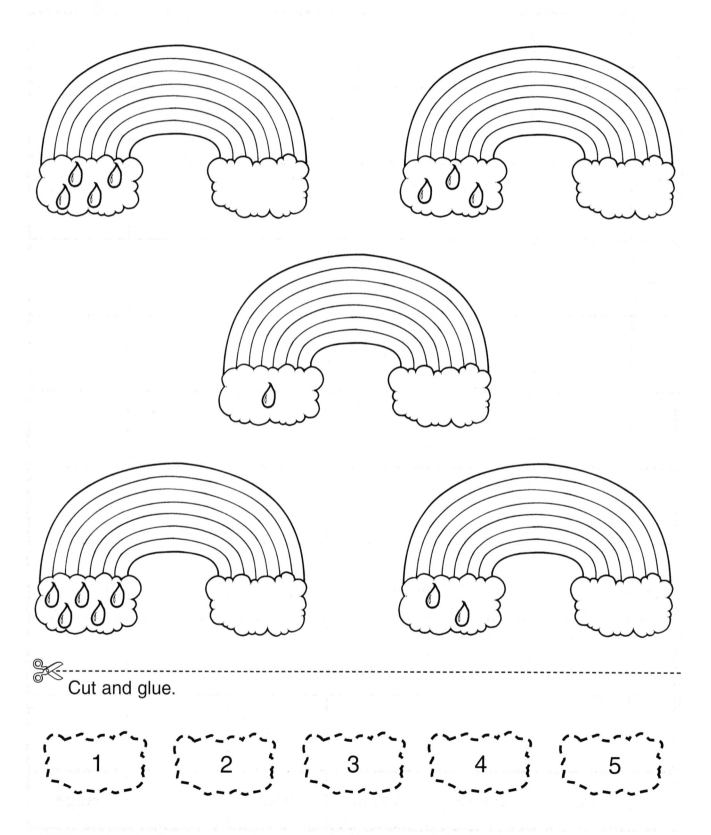

Cut and glue.

38

Colorful Snack Graph

Graph your colorful treats.

10						
9						
8						
7						
6						
5						
4						
3						
2						
1						
	Red	Orange	Yellow	Green	Blue	Purple

Rainbows

White light is made up of all the colors except black, which is the absence of light. Light travels in waves. When white light passes through a prism or raindrops, the wavelengths are bent at different angles. They spread apart into all the colors of the rainbow: red, orange, yellow, green, blue, indigo (deep violet blue), and violet (purple)—(ROY G BIV). Use these two methods to visually demonstrate to your children the order of the rainbow's colors:

Outdoor Rainbow Colors

Materials

- sprinkler or garden hose
- water
- outdoor sunshine

Procedure

The children's backs should be facing the sun. Turn on the sprinkler and create a water mist. Have your children observe the rainbow discovered in the mist. (Caution: Do not allow the children to look directly towards the sun.)

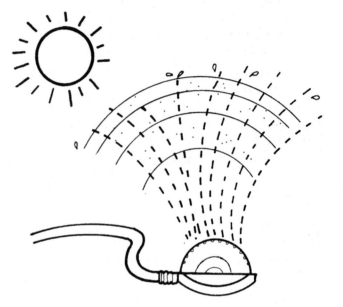

Indoor Rainbow Colors

Materials

- prism
- flashlight
- white wall or a piece of white butcher paper

Procedure

Place the piece of butcher paper on a wall (or use a white wall) to "catch" a rainbow. Shine a flashlight through a prism, aiming the light towards the white paper or on the wall. At the correct angle, a rainbow of color will appear.

Color Delight

You may be able to see a rainbow, but your eyes can be fooled into seeing colors that are not really there. If you stare at a colored image for 30 seconds and then look at a white surface, you will see what is called an *afterimage*. The afterimage has the same shape as the original, but with different colors. For example, when the image is green, the afterimage will be red and vice versa. The technical name for this is successive contrast. Eric Carle's *Hello, Red Fox* (Bibliography, page 79) uses this phenomenon effectively. To make your own afterimage book, cut out simple shapes using different colors of paper. Then using standard sheets of typing paper, create two-sheet "pages." Glue a cut shape to the left side and leave the right side blank. Continue this process for as many shape pages as you'd like to make. Stack the prepared two-sheet pages in the correct sequence, add a front and back cover; bind.

Color Mixing

Color Splash

Materials

- ½ cup (120 mL) 2% or whole milk
- red, yellow, and blue food coloring
- dishwashing detergent
- shallow pan

Directions

- Pour the milk into the pan.
- Add the three colors of food coloring by carefully squeezing a drop of each color in three different areas of the pan.
- Squeeze a small drop of dish detergent into the food coloring areas.
- Observe what happens after the detergent is added.
- Try it a second time, if possible, and make the color droplets closer together so that when the dish washing detergent is added, the colors automatically blend.

Colorful Water

Materials

- four baby food jars (per three children)
- ¼ cup (60 mL) water for each baby food jar
- red, yellow, and blue food coloring

Directions

- Fill the baby food jars with water.
- Have the children predict what they think will happen when two drops of the blue food coloring are added to the water.
- Add the blue food coloring. Ask the children to check their predictions.
- Have them now predict what will happen when they add two drops of the yellow food coloring to the blue food coloring.
- Add the yellow food coloring. Ask the children to check their predictions.
- Repeat the process using the red and yellow food coloring, then using the red and blue food coloring in the second and the third jars.
- In the fourth jar, add two drops of the yellow food coloring and one drop each of the red and the blue food coloring. Have the children make predictions of what color they think it will now make. (Brown)

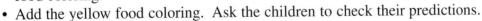

Another Way To Say It

Spanish

Teach your children how to say color names in Spanish. Read *Rainbow Kids* (Bibliography, page 79). The children in this story remember colors from their native Spanish-speaking country, although they now live in the United States.

Red—Rojo/Roja
(rów-ho/rów-ha)

OrangeAnaranjado/Anaranjada
(ah-nah-rahn-háh-tho/ah-nah-rahn-háh-thuh)

Yellow—Amarillo/Amarilla
(ah-mah-ree-yo/ah-mah-ree-ah)

Green—Verde
(véhr-deh)

Blue—Azul
(ah-soól)

Purple—Morado/Morada
(mo-ráh-tho/mo-ráh-thuh)

Black—Negro/Negra
(néh-groh/néh-grah)

White—Blanco/Blanca
(bláhn-koh/bláhn-kah)

Brown—Café
(kah-féh)

Pink—Rosado/Rosada
(row-sáh-tho/row-sáh-thuh)

Chinese

The children of China represent colors using "characters." Teach your children how to say and write their colors using Chinese characters. (Note: In the Chinese language, colors are often referred to as the color of something, for example brown may be "the color of coffee.")

Red
(hung)

Yellow
(hwang)

Green
(leu)

Blue
(lan)

Purple
(zuu)

Black
(he)

Say It With Your Hands, Please!

Teach your children how to sign colors in American Sign Language.

Red		Purple	
Orange		Black	
Yellow		White	
Green		Brown	
Blue		Pink	

Holiday Colors Mini-book

Holiday Colors

Name_____

Colors are a part of our celebrations.

Holiday Colors Mini-book *(cont.)*

Red is the color of the Chinese New Year.

2

Red, pink, and white are the colors of Valentine's Day.

3

Holiday Colors Mini-book (cont.)

Green is the color of St. Patrick's Day.

4

Red, white, and green are the colors of Cinco de Mayo.

5

Holiday Colors Mini-book *(cont.)*

Red, white, and blue are the colors of Independence Day.

6

Black and orange are the colors of Halloween.

7

Holiday Colors Mini-book *(cont.)*

Yellow, orange, and brown are the colors of Thanksgiving.

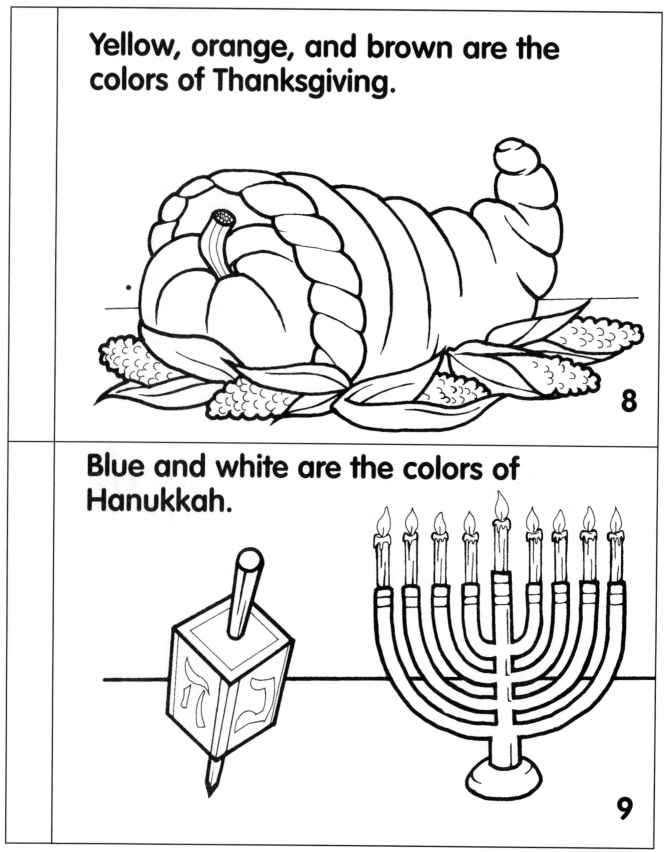

8

Blue and white are the colors of Hanukkah.

9

Holiday Colors Mini-book *(cont.)*

Red and green are the colors of Christmas.

10

Black, red, and green are the colors of Kwanzaa.

11

Color Art

Geometric Shapes

Materials

- pictures of geometric paintings or illustrations (Recommended artist: Piet Mondrian, especially his painting *Composition With Red, Yellow and Blue*)
- several different sizes of square, rectangle, and triangle attribute blocks
- scraps of yellow, red, and blue construction paper
- one 9" x 12" (23 cm x 30 cm) piece of black construction paper
- pencils
- scissors
- glue

Directions

Show the children your selected paintings/illustrations. Point out the artist's use of the primary colors and geometric shapes to create his/her picture. Have the children pick out the shapes that were used. Now explain that they will be creating their own geometric color pictures. Using a pencil and the scrap paper, have them trace around the attribute blocks to create a variety of colored shapes. Cut out the shapes and glue them onto the black construction paper. Encourage the children to use all three primary colors.

Lightest to Darkest

Materials

- sample paint strips from a paint store
- business-sized envelopes

Preparations

Cut the sample strips apart. (Note: Be certain that you somehow label the back of each strip for self-checking purposes.) Place one cut strip into each envelope.

Directions

Have the children practice putting the paint sample colors back in order from lightest to darkest and/or from darkest to lightest.

Mixing Tints and Shades

Materials *(per child)*

- 1 teaspoon (5 mL) each of white, gray, and black tempera paint
- three plastic, self-sealing bags
- 1½ teaspoons (7 mL) of red, orange, yellow, green, blue or purple tempera paints
- one 9" x 12" (23 cm x 30 cm) sheet of white construction paper
- water-filled containers
- paintbrushes

Preparations

Place in each of the three bags, respectively, the white, gray, and black paints.

Directions

1. Have the children predict what colors will be made when they add their chosen paint color to their prepared bags.

2. Allow them to add and mix together their chosen paint colors. Discuss the results.

3. Have the children now paint a picture using the white construction paper and paintbrushes. Display their finished artwork.

Meet the Artist

Eric Carle

Eric Carle was born on June 25, 1929, in Syracuse, New York, to German-American parents.

On the video, *Eric Carle: Picture Writer* (page78), he recalls his kindergarten experiences with painting. He remembers using big brushes and paper and his teacher telling his parents to "nurture" his talent.

He moved to Stuttgart, Germany, when he was in the first grade. He had to deal with learning a new language, a harsh new school, and his homesickness. Soon, he adjusted to his new surroundings and was encouraged by an art teacher.

Carle studied art with Professor Ernst Schneidler at the Akademie der Bildenden Kuenste. He found work easily in his field, beginning with designing posters for a local American information center. After gaining experience, he returned to the United States.

He worked as a designer and art director before becoming a freelance artist. An interest in children's books developed after he agreed to illustrate books written by Bill Martin. Carle revealed, "The child inside me—who had been so suddenly and sharply uprooted and repressed—was beginning to come joyfully back to life."

This joy is evident in Carle's books in his bold, bright colors and original art techniques, playful details, and clever paper engineering. The books he writes have special features such as different paper sizes, crickets chirping and fireflies lighting up at the end of the books, and the ability to trace your own spider web. Mr. Carle has illustrated over sixty books. To see a book list, check out his Web site: www.eric-carle.com

Eric Carle now lives in Northampton, Massachusetts, with his wife, Barbara. He has two adult children.

Eric Carle
P.O. Box 485
Northampton, MA 01060

Tissue-Paper Collage

Materials

- reproduced copies of the Brown Bear pattern (page 18)
- variety of books by and/or illustrated by Eric Carle (see page 51 and page 79)
- *Eric Carle: Picture Writer* (Videotapes, page 78)
- one 9" x 12" (23 cm x 30 cm) piece of blue construction paper
- assorted brown, yellow, and white tissue paper sheets, cut into 1" (2.54 cm) squares
- large paintbrushes
- glue
- crayons, pastels, and/or markers
- scissors
- white glue mixture—one part glue to three parts water
- newspaper to cover work area

Preparations

1. Prepare the tissue-paper sheets by cutting them into 1" (2.54 cm) squares.
2. Mix the white glue mixture.

Directions

1. Discuss how artists, like Eric Carle, illustrate books. Discuss the concept of tissue-paper collages. If desired, show the video at this time.
2. Show books illustrated by Eric Carle; discuss his colorful pages of tissue-paper art.
3. Cover the work surface area with newspaper.
4. Provide each child with a Brown Bear pattern. Have the children cut out the bear and glue to blue construction paper.
5. Have the children use the pre-cut tissue paper in an overlapping fashion inside the lines of the bear on the reproduced pattern.
6. Brush the top surface of the laid-out tissue paper collage with the glue mixture; dry thoroughly.
7. Have the children then add details and textures to their collages using crayons, pastels, and/or markers.

Art Fun

Secondary Hand Prints

Materials

- four shallow pans
- yellow, red, and blue tempera paints
- three 9" x 12" (23 cm x 30 cm) sheets of white construction paper
- water
- paper towels

Directions

1. Place, respectively, the three colors of paint in the three shallow pans and a small amount of water in the fourth pan.

2. Have a child place his/her right hand, palm down, in the yellow paint. Gently press the child's paint-covered hand on the right side of the white construction paper.

3. Place the child's left hand, palm down, in the red paint and then press it gently onto the left side of the white paper.

4. Immediately place the right hand back in the yellow paint and the left hand back in the red paint. Have the child predict what he/she thinks will happen when his/her hands are rubbed together.

5. Have the child gently rub both palms together, mixing the paint thoroughly. Press one hand (left or right) gently in the center of the two previous prints on the white paper. Rinse both hands in the fourth shallow pan filled with water; towel dry.

6. Repeat the process with a second sheet of white paper using the blue and yellow paint. If desired, repeat again with blue and red paint colors.

Mosaics

Materials

- scraps of colored construction paper, pre-cut into 1/2" (1.3 cm) squares
- reproduced Brown Bear Story Props (pages 8–13), one set per child
- scissors
- glue

Directions

Have the children place a thin layer of glue onto the animal shapes. Then, using the paper squares to fill in the pictures, press the squares down gently into the glue using a mosaic (random) placement pattern. When dry, cut out the animals and place them on a background scene made from a large piece of construction paper, chart paper, or small section of bulletin-board paper.

Complementary Paper Weaving

Materials (*per child*)

- one 9" x 12" (23 cm x 30 cm) sheet of either orange, purple, or green construction paper

- nine 1" x 9" (2.54 cm x 23 cm) strips of either yellow, red, or blue construction paper
- glue stick

Materials (*per child*)

Mat Preparations

1. Fold the 9" x 12" (23 cm x 30 cm) sheet of construction paper in half widthwise; keep the paper closed.

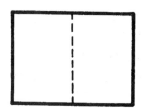

2. Draw parallel pencil lines at 1-inch (2.54 cm) intervals from each of the open-edge sides.

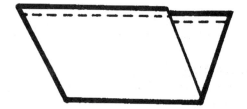

3. Using the pencil lines as a guide, cut desired type of lines* from the fold line to the 1-inch (2.54 cm) width of the bottom edge; open the paper.

   * You may want to use a variety of cut lines (straight, zigzag, curvy, a combination of two or all three) to   add an interesting look to the finished weave.

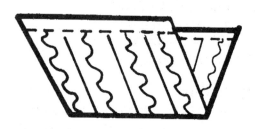

Directions

1. Using the red strips with the prepared green mat (yellow strips with purple mat; blue strips with orange mat), show the children how to paper weave. The first strip goes over and under near the left-side edge, while the second strip, placed next to the first strip, will go under and over. Continue the weaving process until the mat is completed.

2. Glue the ends of the strips to the edges of the mat.

3. If desired, laminate for durability.

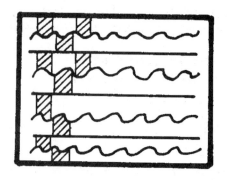

54

Color Songs

Who Stole the Crayons from the Crayon Box?
(Sung to the tune of *Who Stole the Cookies from the Cookie Jar?*)

All of the children: Who stole the crayons from the crayon box?

_____ stole the crayons from the crayon box.
(child's name)

Child: Who me?

All of the children: Yes, you!

Child: Couldn't be!

All of the children: Then who?

All of the children: _____ stole the crayons from the crayon box.

Child: Who me?   (child's name)

All of the children: Yes, you!

Child: Couldn't be!

All of the children: Then who?

(The child names the next child and the chant repeats until all children have a turn.)

Rainbow in the Sky
(Sung to the tune *Twinkle, Twinkle Little Star*)

Rainbow, rainbow in the sky,
I can see you if I try.
After raindrops you will shine,
You are there for me to find.
Rainbow, rainbow in the sky,
Like a painting way up high.

Animals Hiding
(Sung to the tune of *London Bridge is Falling Down*)

Animals are hiding 'round, hiding 'round, hiding 'round
Animals are hiding 'round. Don't disturb them.
They sense many enemies, enemies, enemies.
They sense many enemies. Let's go and hide!
Animals are hiding 'round, hiding 'round, hiding 'round
Animals are hiding 'round. Don't disturb them.

The Artist Paints Pictures
(Sung to the tune of *The Farmer in the Dell*)

The artist paints with red.
The artist paints with red.
Look at all the colors. Oh!
The artist paints with red.
(Repeat as above, simply changing the color name, then finish with the verse below.)

The artist paints pictures.
The artist paints pictures.
Look at all the colors. Oh!
The artist paints pictures.

Very Moving Art!

Color Wheel

Materials

- small carpet mats or chairs for all, but one, of the children

Directions

Assign each child a color of the color wheel: red, orange, yellow, green, blue, or purple. One child is "it." The child who is "it" says one of the colors of the color wheel. The children who have that color must get up and change mats or chairs. The child who is "it" tries to sit on/in one of the emptied mats/chairs. The child who now has no mat/chair is "it." Note: The child who is "it" may also choose to say "color wheel," which means all the children must get up and change their mats or chairs!

Color Relay

Materials

- four small buckets or containers
- forty items, ten of each color: red, green, blue, and orange
- one 9" x 12" (23 cm x 30 cm) sheet each of red, green, blue, and orange construction paper

Directions

1. Mix up all forty items. Randomly place ten items into each of the four buckets. Place the buckets in a straight row forming a "start" line. Place the construction-paper sheets on the ground in a straight line (parallel to the start line), approximately 20 feet (6.06 meters) away. (Note: Make certain the children will not need to "cross paths" when relay begins.)

2. Divide the children into four equal teams. Have each team line up, standing beside their respective bucket. On your signal, one child from each team reaches into their bucket to grab an item. Once the child has decided on the item's predominate color, he/she runs to place it on the appropriate colored sheet of construction paper. The child then runs back to his/her respective team and tags the next person in line. The relay continues until one group has correctly placed all their items and the last team player has returned to the start line. (Variation: Children can also play this game using the complementary colors. In other words, they would place a red item on the green paper and vice versa.)

Colorful Recipes

Strawberry Shortcake

Ingredients (*per child*)

- 2-3 clean strawberries
- 1 teaspoon (5 mL) sugar
- small shortcake
- whipped cream (optional)

Utensils

- sandwich-size self-sealing plastic bags

Directions

Have the children place the clean strawberries and the sugar into their self-sealing bags. Make sure the bags are properly sealed. Have the children squish the ingredients together. After the children have mashed up their strawberries, place the mixture onto the shortcake and top with whipped cream.

Orange Smiles

Ingredients (*per child*)

- one fourth of an orange, peeled into two sections
- 1 teaspoon (5 mL) marshmallow cream
- five mini-marshmallows

Utensils

- butterknife
- napkins

Directions

Separate the two orange sections. Spread a thin layer of marshmallow cream on the sections and place the mini marshmallows between the slices. Put together the slices to form a smile. Place on napkin and serve.

Yellow Pudding Pie

Ingredients

- instant banana pudding
- milk
- graham crackers, crushed
- sliced banana (optional)

Utensils

- serving spoons
- paper plates

Directions

Pour the pudding in an appropriate-sized container and add the milk according to the directions. Have the children mix the pudding until it thickens. Crumble up the graham crackers and add to the pudding. Use a spoon to scoop the pudding onto a paper plate. Top with bananas; serve.

Colorful Recipes *(cont.)*

Green Eggs and Ham

Ingredients

- fresh eggs
- ham, cut into cubes
- green food coloring

Utensils

- bowl
- fork
- microwave-safe bowl

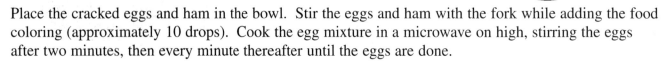

Directions

Place the cracked eggs and ham in the bowl. Stir the eggs and ham with the fork while adding the food coloring (approximately 10 drops). Cook the egg mixture in a microwave on high, stirring the eggs after two minutes, then every minute thereafter until the eggs are done.

Blueberry Muffins

Ingredients

- store-bought blueberry muffin mix
- 1 cup (225g) fresh blueberries, washed and drained

Utensils

- mini-muffin pan
- mini-muffin paper cups
- spatula
- toaster oven

Directions

Preheat the toaster oven as directed on the muffin mix. Prepare the muffins according to the directions on the package. Add the fresh blueberries; fold into the batter. Place the muffin cups in the muffin pan and pour the batter into them. Bake as directed.

Purple Fizz

Ingredients

- vanilla ice cream
- grape soda

Utensils

- ice cream scoop
- small paper cups

Directions

Place a small scoop of ice cream in a small paper cup. Fill up the cup with some grape soda. Enjoy!

58

Colorful Recipes *(cont.)*

Rainbow Fruit and Vegetable Tray

Ingredients
- a variety of colored fruits and vegetables such as strawberries; oranges; bananas; kiwi fruit; blueberries; black, green, or red grapes; cut into bite-size pieces
- skewers (optional)

Directions
Place the fruits and vegetables in an arch to form the colors of the rainbow: red, orange, yellow, green, blue, indigo, and violet. If desired, use the skewers to make a "rainbow on a stick."

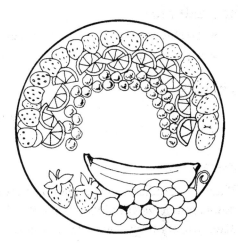

Rainbow in the Sky

Ingredients
- three different kinds of gelatin mix (cherry, grape, and lemon work well)
- whipped cream

Utensils
- gelatin mold
- spoons
- mixing bowl
- measuring cups
- paper plates

Directions
Mix the cherry gelatin according to the directions on the box. Place the gelatin into the mold; allow to gel. Mix the grape gelatin and place on top of the cherry layer; allow to gel. Repeat with the lemon layer. After all three layers have gelled, pop out of the mold and slice. Place each slice on a paper plate and place a dollop of white clouds (whipped cream) on each side to form a rainbow in the sky.

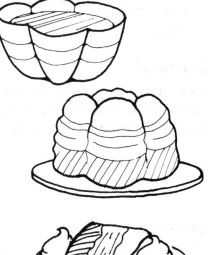

Colorful Recipes (cont.)

Cracker Bear

Ingredients (per child)
- one large, round cracker (If unable to find crackers, use puffed wheat or rice cakes instead.)
- one mini-muffin paper cup holder of peanut butter
- two slices of banana
- two small raisins
- one maraschino cherry half

Utensils (per child)
- napkin
- plastic knife

Directions

As you read the following sequencing poem, your children will be creating an edible bear treat while practicing their listening and sequencing skills! The children's directions are in italic print.

Cracker, cracker, what do you see?
(Places the cracker in front of him/herself on the provided napkin.)

I see peanut butter looking at me!
(Spreads the peanut butter over the cracker's surface using the plastic knife.)

Peanut butter, peanut butter, what do you see? I see two raisin eyes looking at me!
(Children place the two raisins appropriately on top of the peanut butter.)

Raisins, raisins, what do you see? I see banana ears listening to me!
(Children place the two banana slices near the upper edge of the cracker.)

Bananas, bananas, what do you see? I see a red-nosed bear sniffing at me!
(Children place the cherry half on top of the peanut butter.)

Red-nosed bear, red-nosed bear, what do you see? Aaagh! I see a child eating me!
(The children now get to eat their tasty bear treats!)

Color Day Celebration

Get ready, get set, and have a color explosion to end your *Colors* unit. Set up your room into stations that represent all the colors of the rainbow—and more! These activities can also be done on days you may have chosen a specific color-of-the-day.

Set Up

1. Reproduce and send out the donation letter (page 73) requesting any needed items.

2. Ask parents to volunteer as helpers on your Color Celebration Day.

3. Gather all of the needed activity materials (pages 62-67) and food items (recipes, pages 57-60).

4. Place all of the activity materials in labeled baskets so that they will be ready to use and easily switched as your celebration begins.

5. Cover all the tables (stations) with brightly colored butcher paper. You will need one table for recipe creating and six tables for the color activities. (Note: Set aside an area of your room for the children's artwork to dry, rather than taking up room at the station areas.)

6. If you have not done so, make a set of Brown Bear Story Props (page 6, #6) for the children to retell the story at the Revisit the Stories Station.

7. Divide your children into six groups. Plan to have adult helpers lead your children to and through each station.

8. Have the children rotate through the six stations (directions and diagram, page 62).

Color Day Celebration *(cont.)*

Color Stations

Preparations

Divide your children into six groups: A, B, C, D, E, and F. If you have parent helpers, explain each of your chosen stations to them. If no parent helpers are available, explain the stations directly to your children.

Rotating Through the Stations

Each station takes approximately 10 to 20 minutes to complete. At each station, two colors are emphasized, except the last station, which focuses on retelling the featured *Colors* unit literature. If you choose to do all the activities listed, it will take approximately two-and-one-half hours to complete the six stations. A short, three-or-four-minute stretch break between stations is recommended. Let the children know what you will use as a signal to finish up at their station and a second signal to move on to the next one.

Station Red/Orange	Station Black/White	Station Brown/Yellow	Station Green/Blue	Station Purple/Rainbow	Station Revisit the Stories
A	B	C	D	E	F
F	A	B	C	D	E
E	F	A	B	C	D
D	E	F	A	B	C
C	D	E	F	A	B
B	C	D	E	F	A

Color Day Celebration *(cont.)*

Red Station

Materials

- 9" x 12" (23 cm x 30 cm) white construction paper
- red tempera paint
- paintbrushes
- pencils or markers

Directions

Have the children discuss things that are red. After a brainstorming session, have each child paint something different that is predominately red. When finished, they can dictate, or write themselves, something about their drawn item.

Orange Station

Materials

- one part red and two parts yellow modeling play dough—either homemade or store bought
- sandwich-size self-sealing plastic bags (one per child)
- rolling pins
- cookie cutters

Preparations

Make or buy red and yellow modeling play dough. Place one part red dough and two parts yellow dough into each self-sealing bag; seal.

Directions

Have the children predict what color will be made when they mix the two colors of dough. Allow them to mix the two doughs together by squishing their bags. After discussion about what color was made, allow them to roll out their dough and use the cookie cutters to make designs.

Black Station

Materials

- 9" x 12" (23 cm x 30 cm) white construction paper
- thinned-down black tempera paint
- straws
- small plastic flies
- glue
- *Old Black Fly* by Jim Aylesworth (Henry Holt and Company, 1992)

Directions

Read *Old Back Fly*. After discussing the story, have each child place a small amount of black paint in the center of a sheet of white paper. Have them then blow their paint in different directions using the straw. Allow each child to glue a fly on the paper when the paint is dry.

Color Day Celebration *(cont.)*

White Station

Materials

- *It Looks Like Spilt Milk* by Charles G. Shaw (Harper Collins, 1993)
- 9" x 12" (23 cm x 30 cm) blue construction paper
- white tempera paint
- pencils or markers

Directions

Read *It Looks Like Spilt Milk*. After discussing the story, have each child fold a sheet of blue construction paper in half width-wise; crease the fold line and reopen. Have each child then place a small blob of paint near the centerfold line. Have them then refold their papers and press gently. Reopen the papers to discover their spilt-milk clouds! Using the pencils or markers, encourage each child to name their cloud shape and write it on the blue paper.

Brown Station

Materials

- white milk
- liquid chocolate milk syrup
- 8 ounce (240 mL) paper cups
- tablespoon
- craft sticks

Directions

Pour the milk into each cup, about two-thirds full. Allow the children to add two to three tablespoons of chocolate milk syrup to their milk. Stir with the craft sticks and enjoy!

Yellow Station

Materials

- 9" x 12" (23 cm x 30 cm) white construction paper
- pencil
- black permanent markers
- yellow tissue paper, cut into 1-inch (2.54 cm) squares
- glue mixture (one part glue to three parts water)
- paintbrushes

Preparations

Draw a 6-inch (15 cm)-diameter circle in the center of each sheet of white construction paper using the pencil.

Directions

Have the children trace the circle "sun" and add facial details and "rays" of sunshine using the markers. Next, have them place the tissue-paper squares in a collage pattern over their sun. Using the paintbrushes, have them then paint over the squares with the glue mixture; allow to dry.

Color Day Celebration *(cont.)*

Green Station

Materials
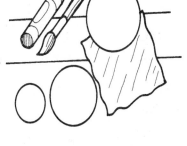

- *Little Blue and Little Yellow* by Leo Lionni (Mulberry Books, 1995)
- 9" x 12" (23 cm x 30 cm) white construction paper
- permanent colored markers
- yellow and blue tissue paper, cut into 6-inch (15 cm)-diameter circles
- glue mixture (one part glue to three parts water)
- paintbrushes

Directions

Read the story. Ask the children to use the colored markers to illustrate their favorite part of the story on the white construction paper. Show them a blue and a yellow tissue-paper circle. Ask the children to predict what color is made when the two colors are put together. Demonstrate the result by overlapping the two pieces of tissue paper. Have the children then place a blue tissue-paper circle and a yellow tissue-paper circle over their illustrations so that just a portion of the two circles are overlapping. Have them then paint the glue mixture over the entire area of both tissue-paper circles; allow to dry.

Blue Station

Materials

- narrow-tip funnel
- one 28 fluid ounces (840 mL) empty dishwashing detergent bottle, with spout
- one cup (225g) flour
- one cup (225g) salt
- one cup (240 mL) water
- blue food coloring
- 9" x 12" (23 cm x 30 cm) sheets of white construction paper
- permanent colored markers

Preparations

Prepare puffy paint by using the funnel to pour the flour and salt into the bottle. Add the water and food coloring (approximately five to seven drops). The paint should be thin enough to pass through the bottle's spout. Pre-make a puffy-paint picture example that highlights blue things for the children to see and touch. (Note: You may need to prepare a second bottle of puffy paint depending on the number of children in your class and how much they draw using the prepared paint.)

Directions

Ask the children to brainstorm things that are blue. After the sharing time, show them your pre-painted picture and share what you think of when you think of blue things. Allow them to touch the dried paint. Have them then paint their own puffy-paint pictures using the construction paper. If desired, have them dictate or write something about their illustrated items using the permanent markers.

Color Day Celebration *(cont.)*

Purple Station

Materials

- *Harold and the Purple Crayon*
  by Crockett Johnson (Harper Collins Publishers,
  1955)
- 9" x 12" (23 cm x 30 cm) white construction paper
- purple crayons

Directions

Read the story. Ask the children what they would draw
with a purple crayon. Ask them to fold their paper into
three sections, accordion-style; unfold and flatten.
Demonstrate what you will want them to do by drawing a
line starting at the far left-side edge of the paper and
bringing the line to the center of the first section. (Do not lift your crayon!) Stop and think about what
you will draw, then draw it. With a continuing stroke, not lifting the crayon from the paper, continue
drawing a line to the second section of the paper. Again, contemplate what you want to draw without
lifting the crayon; draw it and once again, with a continuing motion, draw a line onto the third section;
repeat the process a third time. When finished, fold your paper accordion-style and unfold one section
at a time to reveal the "continuing" illustration. Have the children now create their own continuing
illustrations and share them with each other when completed.

Rainbow Station

Materials

- old CD-ROMs
- sunglasses with "rainbow" film on lenses, if available
- flashlights and prisms (Indoor Rainbow Colors,
  page 40)
- purchased or homemade bubble solution
- various purchased or homemade
  bubble-blowing apparati

Directions

Encourage the children to "see" the rainbows in the CD-
ROMs, glasses, and prisms. Then explain that your
favorite way to see rainbows is in bubbles! Enjoy a
bubble-blowing experience, encouraging the children to tell
you when they can see a rainbow in a bubble.

Color Day Celebration *(cont.)*

Revisit the Stories Station

Note: You may choose one or all three of the book revisit activities. Remember, you will have approximately 20 minutes for this center.

Brown Bear, Brown Bear, What Do You See?

Materials
- a set of Brown Bear Story Props, but using different colors than used in the traditional story (pages 8-13)

Directions

Revisit the story to remind the children of the repetitive text. Then have the children line up with the newly created color sequenced props and retell the story using the new colors.

Mouse Paint

Materials
- reproduced Mouse Colors sheet (page 68)
- red, blue, yellow, purple, orange, and green crayons

Directions

After reading or visually scanning the illustrations of the story, provide each child with a Mouse Colors sheet. Have the children color the first mouse red and its paint puddle yellow. Discuss what color combination that makes, then have them color the palette that color. Repeat with the remaining mice and paint puddles.

They Thought They Saw Him

Materials
- reproduced copies of the chamelon and foliage (pages 28 and 29)
- scissors
- glue
- crayons

Directions

Revisit the illustrations in the story. Then, just for fun, have the children create psychodelic lizards and matching leafy habitats.

Mouse Colors

 +  =

red   yellow

 +  =

blue   red

 +  =

yellow   blue

Bulletin-Board Ideas

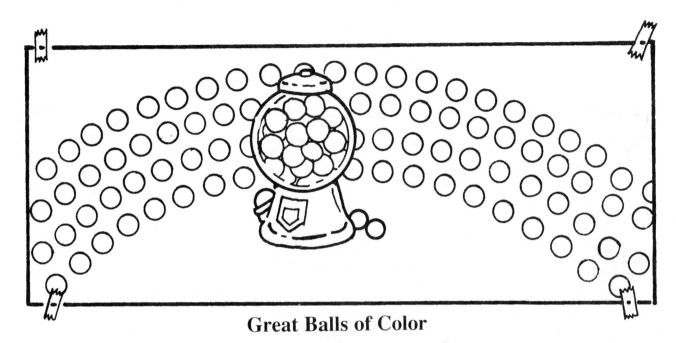

Great Balls of Color

Cover your bulletin-board area with white butcher paper. Enlarge the gumball machine (page 70) using a copying machine with enlarging capabilities or by making a transparency and using an overhead projector. Using brightly colored construction paper, cut out 8-inch (20 cm) circles for the gumball's rainbow arches. Note: Use one color for an entire rainbow arch. If desired, label each row's color with its color name.

I Thought I Saw Him

Copy the chameleon pattern (page 28) onto a sheet of brightly colored construction paper, matching it to one of the colors in your gumball machine bulletin-board display (above). Cut out the lizard and attach it to a pointer stick or unsharpened pencil. Show the children how a chameleon or anole uses its color to hide from its prey and enemies by placing it against the rainbow's gumballs; discuss their discoveries.

Gumball Machine Pattern

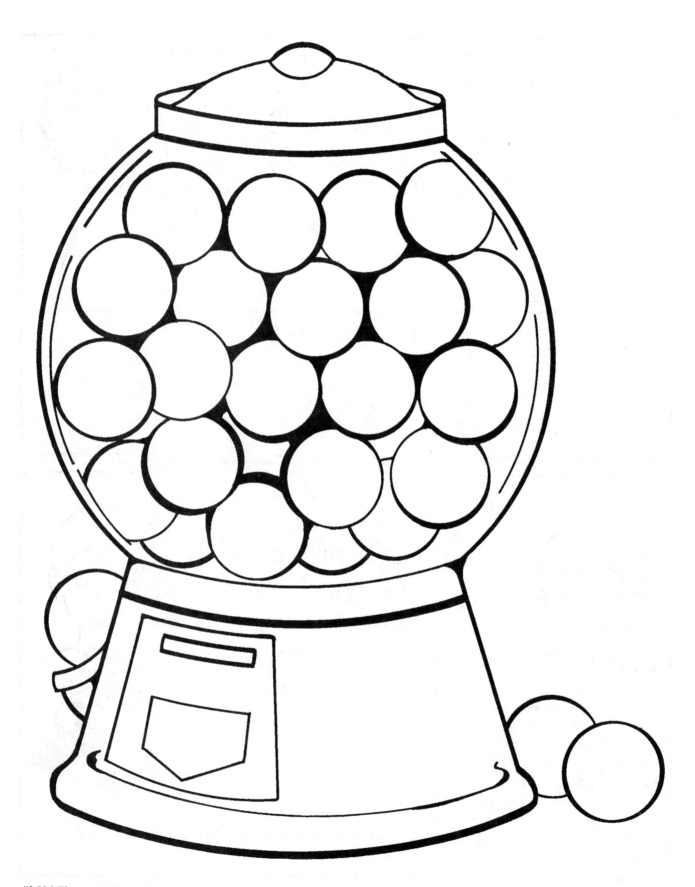

Messy Day Letter and Certificate

A Messy Day
is
Coming Our Way

on _____
Date

when we will be

_____
Messy Activity

I am proud
as I can be,

I know my colors!
Hurray for me!

Name_____   Date _____

Bookmark and Ribbon

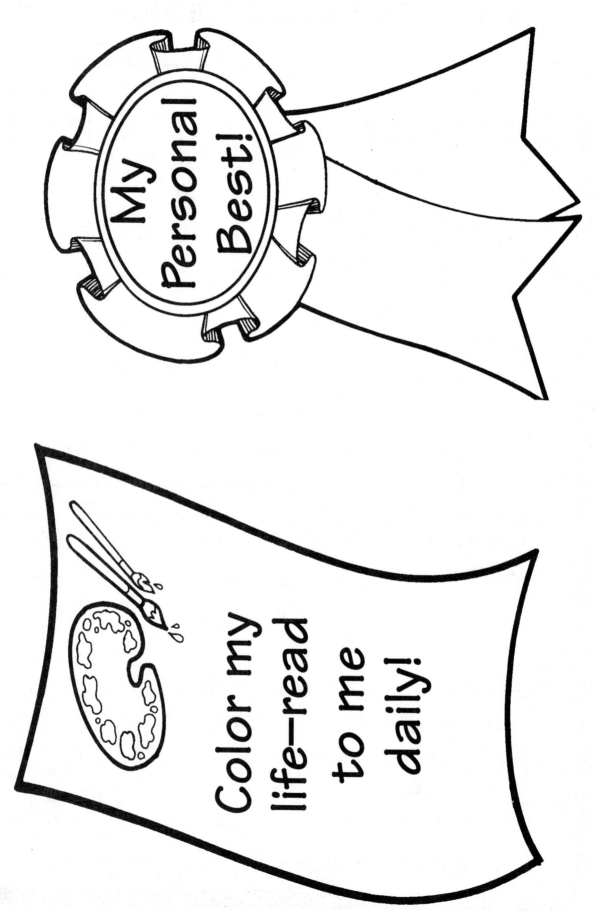

Donation Letter

Dear Family,

We have been learning about the colors all around us. We want to celebrate what we have learned by having a Color Day Celebration on _____ at _____ !

                   (date)   (time)

We will be wearing our favorite color clothing, eating different colors of food, and making colorful crafts! To help our celebration be successful, we need the following items:

_____

_____

_____

_____

_____

Please send them in by_____

If you would like to help with the color celebration stations, please let me know by filling out the form below. I appreciate your help!

Thank you,

✂ -

Name of child _____ Phone Number _____

Caregiver's Name _____

I can help on the day of the Color Day Celebration.   Yes   No

                                                                 (circle one)

I can donate these items: _____

_____

Color Basics

Portfolios

All great artists use portfolios to keep their work neat and ready to show off their masterpieces! Create these easy portfolios for your children's artwork.

Materials *(per child)*

- colorful file folder
- scissors
- reproduced copy of page 75 (onto tagboard)
- stapler
- glue
- crayons, colored pencils, or markers

Preparations

1. Cut the tab off the file folder so that it is a rectangular shape.
2. Attach the reproduced handles with a stapler.
3. Glue the nametag on the front of the file-folder portfolio.

Directions

Have the children put their name on their portfolios and decorate them with crayons. Keep the prepared portfolios in a file box for easy storage.

Palettes

Another tool an artist uses is a palette for mixing paints. Use white paper plates to make palettes for the children to use while enjoying a painting project.

Brushes

Teach the children how to take care of paintbrushes. Explain to them that an artist takes care of his/her paintbrushes by cleaning them after each use and by not pushing down on the bristles. Demonstrate how to properly use and clean a paintbrush. If you will be using a variety of sizes and shapes, you may want to color code the handles so that the children can place them in matching color-coded containers at clean-up time.

Art Box

Allow each child to create an art box using an empty shoebox to hold his/her art supplies. Here are suggestions for items to put in the boxes:

- regular pencils
- colored pencils
- watercolors
- crayons
- colored chalk
- tempura paints
- paintbrushes
- pencil sharpeners
- erasers
- palettes
- rulers
- glue
- scissors
- stamps
- stencils
- sponges

Art Smocks

Have the children bring oversized T-shirts or men's dress shirts from home to wear as art smocks to protect their clothing when painting.

74

Portfolio

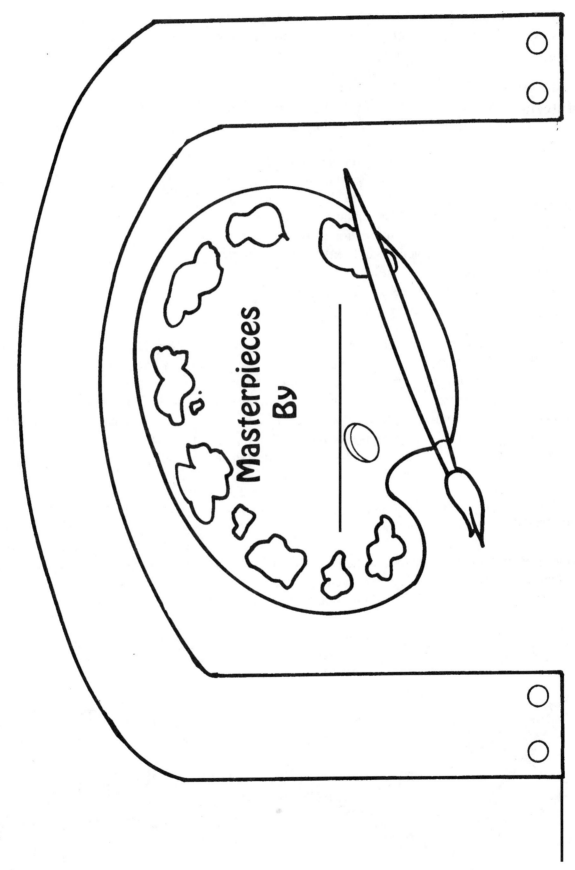

Masterpieces
By

Color and the Wheel

"Color" is one of the art elements that young children can experience with instant success. The art activities in this unit will teach your children about the color wheel, primary colors, secondary colors, shades, tones and tints, and complementary colors.

Artists use the *color wheel* as a guide to see the relationships between colors. The basic color wheel shows the primary, secondary, intermediate, and complementary colors.

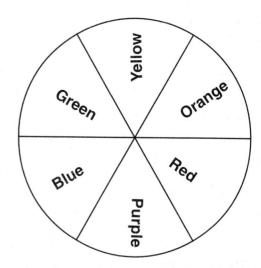

The *primary colors* (red, yellow, and blue) can not be created with any other colors. These colors, when mixed together in certain combinations, create all colors. The primary colors are placed in a triangle formation on an artist color wheel. The *secondary colors* are a combination of two primary colors mixed together. Orange (yellow and red), purple (blue and red), and green (yellow and blue) are known as the secondary colors. The order of the wheel, going clockwise, is yellow, orange, red, purple, blue, and green.

The *intermediate colors* are a combination of primary and secondary colors. They are placed on the color wheel between the two mixed colors. *Complementary colors* are colors directly opposite each other on the color wheel. Purple and yellow are complementary colors because of their placement on the color wheel. Artists know that using complementary colors will emphasize the colors in their paintings. Placing complementary colors next to each other make each color more vivid and make the picture seem to vibrate with its opposite. Artists are not the only ones who know the effect of placing complementary colors together. Food-store advertisers use this concept to bring out their products; an example of this would be strawberries in a green basket.

The colors black, white, and gray are called *neutral colors*. *Warm colors* are yellow, red, and orange. *Cool colors* are blue, purple, and green.

Shades, tones, and tints are used to help an artist create a 3-D look to a painting. *Shades* are made by adding black paint to any color to darken it. *Tones* are made with any color and gray mixed together. *Tints* are the opposite of shades. With tints, white paint is added to lighten any color.

This information is designed to help in your color explanations. Depending on your children's age levels and exposure to art concepts will affect how much will be shared.

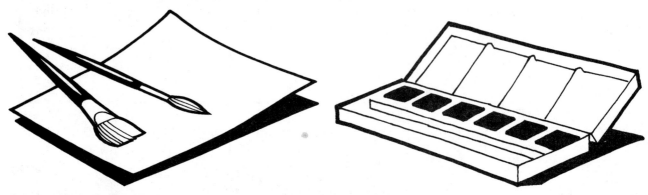

Web Sites

The Web sites listed here will help you gain information about color, provide pages to print, gives you on-line coloring pages for those linked to the Internet, and color/holiday activities for your children to complete.

Exploratorium

www.exploratorium.edu/ti/resources/lightandcolor.html
Books, videos, and other sites pertaining to light and color are found at this site.

Can Teach

persweb.direct.ca/ikhan/elementary/songspoems.html
Wonderful color (and holiday) songs and poems to delight your children can be found at this site.

Child Fun

www.childfun.com/themes/color.shtml
Color activities galore awaits you at this Web site!

Kids Domain

www.kidsdomain.com/holidays/index.html
Coloring pages, puzzles, and craft activities for the holidays are provided.

Kinder Art

www.kinderart.com/painting/
Here you can find painting activities for active little hands.

The Official Eric Carle Web Site

www.eric-carle.com/
This site has a list of books by Eric Carle, a short biography, and links to his hometown.

Pre-School Fun Zone

www.angelfire.com/fl/preschoolfunzone/
This site has color day activities, songs, arts and crafts, and holiday fun.

To Nuttin' But Kids

www.vbe.com/~gns/colors.html
Group activities pertaining to color, including songs, chants, and arts and crafts are available at this location.

Multimedia

Videotapes

Amazing Animals: Animal Colors. DK Vision and Partridge Films, 1997. Approximately 30 minutes.

Amazing Animals: Animal Disguises. DK Vision and Partridge Films, 1996. Approximately 30 min.

Colors! DK Vision—Dorling Kindersley Ltd., 1995. 30 minutes.

Eric Carle: Picture Writer. Scholastic, 1993. 27 minutes.

Hailstones and Halibut Bones. AIMS Media, 1993. 15 minutes.

Reptiles and Insects. Walt Disney Home Video, 1995. Approximately 25 minutes each section.

Computer Software

Blue's Treasure Hunt. CD ROM. Viacom International Inc., 1999. Macintosh and Windows. Ages 3-6.

Crayola—Magic 3D Coloring Book. CD ROM. International Business Machines Corporation, 1999. Windows 98/95. Ages 3-7.

Disney's Magic Artist Studio. CD ROM. Disney Interactive, Inc., 500 S. Buena Vista Blvd., Burbank, CA 91521. Macintosh and Windows 98/95. All Ages.

Elmo's Art Workshop. CD ROM. Learning Company Properties, Inc., 1998. Windows 98/95/3.1 and Macintosh. Ages 2-6.

Kid Pix. CD ROM. The Learning Company, 1999. 500 Redwood Blvd., Novato, CA 94948-6121. (415) 382-4400. Macintosh and Windows 98/95/3.1. Ages 3-12.

Maisy's Playhouse. CD ROM. Sound Source Interactive, Inc. and Simon & Schuster Interactive, 1999. Macintosh and Windows. All ages. www.soundssourceinteractive.com

Music

Greg & Steve. *Playing Favorites.* "Brown Bear, Brown Bear, What Do You See?" 1991. Youngheart Music Inc., P.O. Box 6017, Cypress, CA 90630-0017. 1-800-444-4287.

Greg & Steve. *We All Live Together,* Volume 2. "The World is a Rainbow" Little House Music, 1978. CTP/ Youngheart, P.O. Box 6017, Cypress, CA 90630-0017. 1-800-444-4287.

Palmer, Hap. *Learning Basic Skills Through Music Volume I.* "Colors" Educational Activities, Inc., 1994. Educational Activities, Inc. Box 392 Dept. AS, Freeport, NY 11520. 1-800-645-3739.

Palmer, Hap. *Learning Basic Skills Through Music Volume II.* "Parade of Colors" Educational Activities, Inc., 1995. Educational Activities, Inc., Box 392 Dept. AS, Freeport, NY 11520. 1-800-645-3739.

Phil Rosenthal and Family. *The Green Grass Grew All Around.* "The Green Grass Grew All Around" American Melody, 1995. American Melody, P.O. Box 270, Guilford, CT 06437.

Bibliography

Fiction

Anholt, Catherine. *Tom's Rainbow Walk.* Little, Brown and Company, 1989.

Aruego, Jose and Ariane Dewey. *The Lizard's Song.* Greenwillow, 1979.

Aruego, Jose and Ariane Dewey. *We Hide, You Seek.* Greenwillow, 1979.

Asch, Frank. *Skyfire.* Simon and Schuster Books, 1984.

Bang, Molly. *The Grey Lady and the Strawberry Snatcher.* Four Winds Press, 1980.

Bernhard, Drog. *Alphabeasts.* Holiday House, 1993.

Blackstone, Stella. *Can You See the Red Balloon?* Orchard Books, 1997.

Cabrera, Jane. *Cat's Colors.* Dial Books for Young Readers, 1997.

Carle, Eric. *Hello, Red Fox.* Simon & Schuster, 1998.

Carle, Eric. *The Mixed-up Chameleon.* Harper Collins, 1975.

Crews, Donald. *Ten Black Dots.* Greenwillow, 1986.

dePaola, Tomie. *The Art Lesson.* G.P. Putnam's Sons, 1989.

dePaola, Tomie. *Charlie Needs a Cloak.* Scholastic, 1978.

Dodds, Dayle Anne. *The Color Box.* Little, Brown and Company, 1992.

Ehlert, Lois. *Color Zoo.* J.B. Lippincott, 1989.

Ehlert, Lois. *Planting a Rainbow.* J.B. Lippincott, 1989.

Emberly, Ed. *Go Away Big Green Monster.* Little, Brown and Company, 1992.

Ernst, Lisa. *The Bee.* Lothrop, Lee & Shepard Books, 1986.

Fernandez, Mayra. *Rainbow Kids.* DDL Books, Inc., 1995.

Freeman, Don. *A Rainbow of My Own.* Puffin Books, 1978.

Freeman, Don. *The Chalk Box Story.* J.B. Lippincott Company, 1976.

Gibbons, Gail. *The Art Box.* Holiday House, Inc., 1998.

Henkes, Kevin. *Lilly's Purple Plastic Purse.* Greenwillow Books, 1996.

Hoban, Tana. *Colors Everywhere.* Greenwillow Books, 1995.

Hoban, Tana. *Is it Red? Is it Yellow? Is it Blue?* Greenwillow Books, 1978.

Hoban, Tana. *Of Colors and Things.* Mulberry Books, 1989.

Hubbard, Patricia. *My Crayons Talk.* Henry Holt and Company, 1996.

Jackson, Ellen. *Brown Cow, Green Grass, Yellow Mellow Sun.* Hyperion Books for Children, 1995.

Jenkins, Jessica. *Thinking About Colors.* Dutton Children's Books, 1992.

Jonas, Ann. *Color Dance.* Greenwillow Books, 1989.

Kim, Joy. *Rainbows and Frogs.* Troll Associates, 1981.

Kunhardt, Edith. *Red Day, Green Day.* Greenwillow Books, 1992.

Levinson, Riki. *Country Dawn to Dusk.* Dutton Children's Books, 1992.

Lionni, Leo. *A Color of His Own.* Alfred A. Knopf, 1975.

Lionni, Leo. *Little Blue and Little Yellow.* Mulberry Books, 1995.

Mallat, Kathy. *The Picture That Mom Drew.* Walker Publishing, 1997.

Bibliography *(cont.)*

McCloskey, Robert. *Blueberries for Sal.* Viking, 1948.

McMillan, Bruce. *Growing Colors.* Lothrop, Lee & Shepard Books, 1988.

Serfozo, Mary. *Who Said Red?* Macmillian Publishing Company, 1988.

Seuss, Dr. *Green Eggs and Ham.* Random House, 1960.

Seuss, Dr. *My Many Colored Days.* Random House, 1996.

Spinelli, Eileen. *If You Want to Find Golden.* Albert Whitman & Company, 1993.

Swinburne, Stephen. *Lots and Lots of Zebra Stripes.* Boyds Mill Press, 1998.

VanLeen, Nancy. *Rainbow Crow.* Knopf, 1989.

Weitzman, Jacqueline Preiss and Robin Preiss Glasser. *You Can't Take a Balloon Into The Metropolitan Museum.* Dial Books for Young Readers, 1998.

West, Tracey. *Liz Makes a Rainbow.* Scholastic, 1999.

Williams, Sue. *I Went Walking.* Gulliver Books, 1989.

Wilson, April. *April Wilson's Magpie Magic: A Tale of Colorful Mischief.* Dial Books for Young Readers, 1999.

Wood, Don and Audrey Wood. *The Little Mouse, The Red Ripe Strawberry, and The Big Hungry Bear.* Child's Play (International) Ltd., 1984.

Yamaka, Sara. *The Gift of Driscoll Lipcomb.* Simon & Schuster, 1995.

Nonfiction

Arnosky, Jim. *I See Animals Hiding.* Scholastic Inc., 1995.

Dewey, Ariane. *Naming Colors.* HarperCollins, 1995.

Ganeri, Anita. *Animals in Disguise.* Little Simon, 1995.

Mara, W.P. *Anoles.* Capstone Press, 1996.

Mara, W.P. *Chameleons.* Capstone Press, 1996.

Martin, James. *Hiding Out: Camouflage in the Wild.* Crown Publishers, Inc., 1993.

Martin, Terry. *Why Are Zebras Black and White?* DK Publishing, 1991.

Perry, Phyllis J. *Hide and Seek: Creatures in Camouflage.* Frankin Watts, 1997.

Powzyk, Joyce. *Animal Camouflage.* Bradbury Press, 1990.

Souza, D.M. *Catch Me If You Can.* Carolrhoda Books, Inc., 1992.

Westray, Kathleen. *A Color Sampler.* Tickner & Fields, 1993.

Yenawine, Philip. *Colors.* Delacorte Press, 1991.

Poetry

O'Neill, Mary. *Hailstones and Halibut Bones.* Doubleday, 1961.

Rossetti, Christina. *Color.* Harper Collins Publishers, 1992.